UK 8/17

PERSPECTIVES ON
EUROPEAN COLONIZATION OF AMERICA

by Clara MacCarald

12 STORY LIBRARY

www.12StoryLibrary.com

Copyright © 2018 by 12-Story Library, Mankato, MN 56003. All rights reserved. No part of this book may be reproduced or utilized in any form or by any means without written permission from the publisher.

12-Story Library is an imprint of Bookstaves and Press Room Editions

Produced for 12-Story Library by Red Line Editorial

Photographs ©: North Wind Picture Archives, cover, 1, 4, 5, 7, 9, 10, 13, 20, 24, 25, 28; Dmitry Trubitsyn/Shutterstock Images, 6; Townsend MacCoun/Lionel Pincus and Princess Firyal Map Division/New York Public Library, 8; Zbigniew Guzowski/Shutterstock Images, 11; NativeStock/North Wind Picture Archives, 12; MPI/Archive Photos/Getty Images, 14; Bain News Service/George Grantham Bain Collection/Library of Congress, 15; Detroit Photographic Co/Photochrom Print Collection/Library of Congress, 16; dmvphotos/Shutterstock Images, 17; Gerry Embleton/North Wind Picture Archives, 19; Everett Historical/Shutterstock Images, 22, 23; Edward S. Curtis/Edward S. Curtis Collection/Library of Congress, 26; Kobby Dagan/Shutterstock Images, 27; Jorg Hackemann/Shutterstock Images, 29

Content Consultant: Jacob F. Lee, Assistant Professor, History Department, Indiana University–Bloomington

Library of Congress Cataloging-in-Publication Data
A catalog record for this book is available from the Library of Congress
978-1-63235-400-6 (hardcover)
978-1-63235-472-3 (paperback)
978-1-62143-524-2 (ebook)

Printed in the United States of America
022017

Access free, up-to-date content on this topic plus a full digital version of this book. Scan the QR code on page 31 or use your school's login at 12StoryLibrary.com.

Table of Contents

Fact Sheet

What started European colonization of America?

In the 1500s and 1600s, many colonists came from several European countries. The colonists came to America for various reasons. Many sought profit. Others wanted a new life. At first, they competed with one another to trade with certain American Indian tribes for furs. Soon colonists claimed land for their home countries.

What happened during European colonization?

Many American Indian tribes, such as the Wyandots, sought out relationships with Europeans. They wanted to trade goods. The colonists brought new things to America. They brought manufactured goods, such as metal cooking pots. They brought animals and plants from Europe that American Indians had never seen.

What changed because of European colonization?

Some American Indian tribes came to rely on European goods. As they used them more, fewer people followed traditional ways. The fur trade made ongoing conflicts among tribes even worse. Wars between American Indian tribes and wars with colonists pushed some groups off their lands.

American Indian tribes and European colonists had different views on land ownership. American Indian tribes believed land belonged to a group. Europeans believed land was owned by individual people. Sometimes American Indian tribes thought they made agreements to share land, but colonists believed they had bought it. There were times when tribes came together to try to defend their land.

Europeans changed the land. They cut trees, planted new crops, and let their livestock wander. They also brought new illnesses. Vast numbers of American Indians died due to disease and war. The number of colonists continued to increase.

French Come to the New World Seeking Furs

Some French explorers and fishers came to North America in the early 1500s. They began to trade with American Indian tribes, such as the Micmacs in modern-day Maine. The Frenchmen gave American Indians things made in Europe, such as guns, metal cooking pots, and beads. The American Indians gave the French furs in return. Furs were expensive in Europe. Soon the French were making a lot of money.

The French traders sailed the St. Lawrence River from the coast of Canada inland toward the Great Lakes. They were welcomed by tribes such as the Wyandots and Ottawas. The tribes supplied the French with furs, especially ones from beavers. Hats made from beavers are very warm. Beaver hats were also very fashionable in Europe in the 1600s. Mounds of beaver fur crossed the Atlantic to be sold in Europe.

French traders came to North America looking for furs like these.

French traders often used boats to transport the furs.

The fur trade helped make some conflicts between American Indian tribes worse. By dealing with specific tribes, the French made local enemies. One enemy was the powerful Haudenosaunee Confederacy, made up of five Iroquois-speaking tribes. They made it hard for other American Indians to bring furs to French trading posts.

The French tried to protect their trade, but attacks from the Haudenosaunee continued. Around 1650, the Haudenosaunee Confederacy pushed French trading partners off their land. The Eries went south toward North Carolina and South Carolina. The Ottawas and the Wyandots went west. The French fur traders followed them inland.

85

Number of colonists in New France in 1627.

- French traders came looking for furs.
- French traders worked and exchanged European goods with some American Indian tribes, such as the Wyandots and Ottawas.
- By dealing with certain tribes, the French became enemies of the Haudenosaunee Confederacy.
- French traders moved inland to follow their trading partners.

Dutch Try to Compete for Trade

The Dutch West India Company started in 1621. Its purpose was to trade with parts of Africa and the Americas. But company workers also raided Spanish ships, which were bringing treasures from Spanish colonies in America.

To enter the fur trade, Dutch colonists settled land along the Hudson River in what is now New York State. This area, called New Netherland, grew slowly.

The Dutch could make more money by raiding.

The Dutch West India Company decided colonists should settle farms. These could supply the merchants with food while protecting the company's trade. Many European countries wanted to control the fur trade. The French tried to persuade the Haudenosaunee Confederacy to trade with them instead of the Dutch. English and Swedish colonists struggled with the Dutch for the best locations for trading posts.

Sometimes colonists bought land from local tribes. They exchanged small amounts of goods for large amounts of land. Sometimes the colonists claimed territory without payment.

Because not many people from their own country wanted to move to the colonies, the Dutch accepted

Map of New Amsterdam in New Netherland, which is now Manhattan, New York

52,584

Number of beaver furs the Dutch sent back to the Netherlands from 1626 to 1632.

- The Dutch came to the New World looking for fur.
- Farms supplied Dutch merchants with food and helped protect their trade.
- Some colonists bought territory from American Indians, but many colonists claimed land without payment.
- The English took over the Dutch colonies.

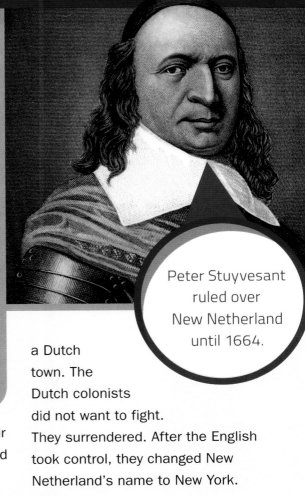

Peter Stuyvesant ruled over New Netherland until 1664.

settlers from many nations. But their English neighbors soon outnumbered the Dutch colonists. One day in 1664, English warships approached a Dutch town. The Dutch colonists did not want to fight. They surrendered. After the English took control, they changed New Netherland's name to New York.

INTO THE WOODS

Some French and Dutch traders did business directly with American Indians. They did not wait to trade at legal trading posts. In French, they were called *coureurs de bois*, or "runners of the woods." These traders were successful because they adopted the customs of many American Indian tribes. They canoed to find Native villages. They learned Native languages and ways. The runners of the woods were happy to sell their traded furs to whoever paid the highest price, even if it was against the law.

Virginia Sees Opportunity in Tobacco

English settlers arrived in Virginia in 1607 with support from the Virginia Company of London. To make a profit, the settlers hoped to find gold. Some wanted to raid Spanish ships for precious metals, while others wanted to mine. The colonists believed they deserved to take over land American Indians had been living on for centuries. But doing so proved hard. Supplies for the colony kept running out.

Settlers expected American Indians to provide them with corn. Some tribes sometimes did. Other times, the local tribes attacked them. Conflict grew between the English and the powerful Powhatan Confederacy that lived in the area. Hunger, disease, and war killed many settlers.

The people of Jamestown wanted to search for gold instead of growing

Colonists had to bring all their supplies with them to the New World.

food. They found a shiny rock they thought might contain gold. They gathered up enough to fill a ship. The ship brought the rocks to England. There, people discovered the rock was worthless. The colonists sold other goods but made very little money for the company.

Colonists wanted to abandon Jamestown. But things turned around when they started growing tobacco. It grew well in Virginia. Europeans had developed a taste for it. The colonists could sail from the Chesapeake Bay to ship tobacco back to England.

The colonists began to make a profit. Their success lured new colonists to come. Tobacco production needed a lot of land. The colonists grabbed as much territory as they could. The Powhatans resisted, but the English hit back. Some colonists were happy having an excuse to drive the tribes out of the area.

Tobacco grew well in Virginia but did not prosper in New England.

60,000
Approximate number of pounds (27,000 kg) of tobacco shipped from Virginia in 1620.

- English colonists came to Virginia to make money.
- Settlers found hunger and hard work instead.
- Settlers began to make money when they started farming tobacco.
- To grow more tobacco, the settlers took away land that belonged to the Powhatans.

Powhatan Tries to Contain Jamestown

Chief Powhatan ruled about 30 Algonquin-speaking tribes near the Chesapeake Bay in what is now the state of Virginia. Most of the tribes he conquered himself. In 1607, the English founded a town near the bay. They called it Jamestown. The English had metal tools and guns. Chief Powhatan wanted to rule the English as well.

His people captured a leading colonist, Captain John Smith. Powhatan adopted him as a lower chief.

To do so, his people held a feast. Then they pretended to prepare to kill Smith. They stopped the execution at the last minute. After this ritual, Smith belonged to the Powhatan Confederacy.

Smith returned to Jamestown. But he misunderstood what had

Replicas of Powhatan homes outside the Jamestown Settlement in Virginia

6
Number of tribes Powhatan started with.

- Chief Powhatan ruled many tribes near the Chesapeake Bay.
- Powhatan wanted to add Jamestown to his empire.
- Fighting between the Powhatans and the colonists let up after Pocahontas married an Englishman.
- After Chief Powhatan died, the Powhatans lost most of their land to the English.

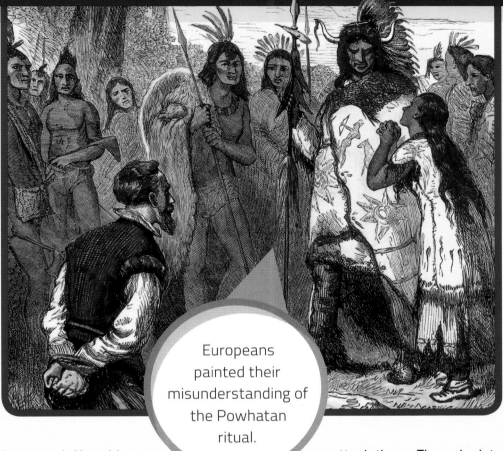

Europeans painted their misunderstanding of the Powhatan ritual.

happened. He told other colonists the execution had been real. He believed Powhatan's daughter Pocahontas saved him. Smith wanted to make Powhatan part of the English empire. He gave Powhatan royal presents and placed a crown on his head.

Neither the English nor the Powhatans bowed down to each other. Chief Powhatan continued to trade with the colonists. Sometimes, though, he had some of his people attack them. The colonists sometimes angered the Powhatans by demanding food.

Relations between the Powhatans and settlers improved when Pocahontas agreed to marry a colonist. Peace lasted for a few years. Then Powhatan died. His brother wanted to destroy the English. The conflict killed many. More colonists arrived. Very few Powhatans survived the fighting. They lost almost all their lands to the colonists.

Munsees Try to Share Land

For hundreds of years, the Munsees lived in small towns in the US Northeast. They farmed and gathered food from the forest. Munsee groups did not share a government. They were connected by friendship and blood. People moved among the groups and even nearby tribes to marry.

The Dutch arrived to trade in the 1600s. The Munsees exchanged fur, supplies, and information for European goods. They began to depend on metal tools instead of stone ones.

At first, the Dutch traders came and went back to Europe with the furs. Then they offered to buy Munsee land, such as Manhattan and Staten Island. But the Munsees did not think they were selling the land forever.

The Munsees later signed a treaty with the US government, giving up land.

Like other American Indian nations, individual Munsee people did not own land. Their tribe held territory. Families and clans had the right to use it. They needed land for farming and hunting. The Munsees thought the Dutch would share the land in exchange for trade goods. They also expected the Dutch to be their allies.

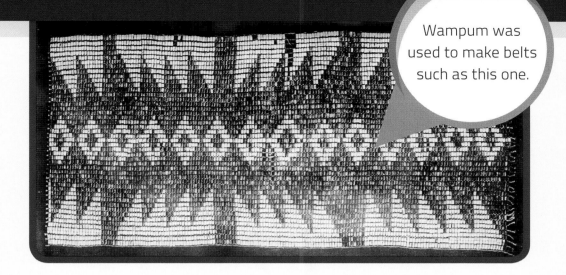

Wampum was used to make belts such as this one.

The Munsees continued to live on their land. Peace didn't last. The Dutch demanded food. Settlers' cattle trampled Munsee gardens and damaged their homes.

War broke out. Many Munsees died before they agreed to stop fighting. European diseases such as the flu and smallpox killed many more. Settlers and war pushed many of the surviving Munsees out of their homeland.

WAMPUM TRADE

The Munsees and other American Indians traded long before meeting the Dutch. Northern groups, such as the Haudenosaunee, particularly prized wampum. Wampum is a kind of bead. Tribes that lived along the coast, such as the Munsees, made them from shells. Wampum had sacred and political uses. The wampum trade increased when Europeans arrived. Using metal tools, people could make the beads even faster.

2,500
Estimated number of Munsees living in the late 1600s.

- The Munsees lived in towns in the Northeast.
- When the Dutch bought land, Munsee leaders thought they were sharing it.
- Many Munsees who survived war and disease were forced to move.

Haudenosaunee Confederacy Faces Enemies

Before most European colonists arrived in the United States, the Haudenosaunee Confederacy formed. The prophet Deganawida and his follower Hiawatha convinced five Iroquois tribes to unite under one government. The group was also called the Iroquois League or Five Nations.

The Confederacy brought peace to the Haudenosaunees. But the group sometimes fought with outside tribes. Some of these groups shared the same culture but had refused to join the Confederacy.

When the Dutch arrived, the Confederacy began trading beaver furs for Dutch goods. The Haudenosaunees started to rely on European metal and tools. Eventually, they killed so many beavers that they needed more land for hunting. The Confederacy fought with other American Indian nations to take their lands. These conflicts took place from the 1630s to 1700 and are known as the Beaver Wars.

In addition to land, the Confederacy also needed people. Many had died from a European disease called

Europeans later imagined what Hiawatha looked like.

GUNS CHANGE WAR

Guns from the 1600s were not much more effective than bows. Loading a gun took time, while warriors could shoot many arrows quickly. Often, bullets did not hit what they were aimed at. But bullets pierced the nonmetal armor and shields used by American Indians. Guns made war deadlier. Warriors had to take cover rather than fight face-to-face.

smallpox. The Haudenosaunees defeated the Wendat nation by 1650 and took many captives. They made the captives part of the Confederacy. When the English took over the Dutch colonies, the Confederacy began an uneasy relationship with them.

50
Number of chiefs in the Haudenosaunee Confederacy.

- Five American Indian nations banded together to form the Haudenosaunee Confederacy.
- The Confederacy made peace with each other, but fought wars with outsiders.
- The Confederacy provided the Dutch with furs, but overhunting caused the Haudenosaunees to take part in the Beaver Wars.

Old guns such as this replica could hold only one bullet at a time.

Wyandots Make a New Home

During the Beaver Wars, the Haudenosaunee Confederacy pushed some American Indians from their homelands. The Eries escaped south and became known as the Westos. Some survivors formed new groups, such as the Wyandots, which included Wendats, and Tionontati. Others joined existing groups, such as the Ottawas. The Wyandots settled new homes around the St. Lawrence River and the Great Lakes.

There the Wyandots and Ottawas met the Great Lakes tribes. Some Great Lakes tribes, such as the Miami (Myaamia) and the Illinois Confederacy, were unfamiliar with European goods. This created new opportunities for trade. For example, the Ottawas traded with the Great Lakes tribes for furs. Then the Ottawas brought the furs to French trading posts.

In 1701, communities around the Great Lakes made peace with the Haudenosaunee Confederacy. The Wyandots invited other groups to the area. Some had fled wars or had lost their lands to settlers. Many people from different tribes lived and worked closely together.

261
Number of French soldiers around the Great Lakes in 1750.

- Some American Indian nations fled to the Great Lakes during the Beaver Wars.
- They continued trading with the French and began trading with other local tribes.
- In 1754, the Wyandots and the Ottawas fought in the war between the French and English.

Peace did not last. The French and English went to war in 1754. American Indian groups took sides. The Wyandots and Ottawas allied with the French. But the English won the war in 1763.

The Wyandots and the Ottawas fought alongside their trading partners.

The English promised tribes that settlers would stop moving west. But that promise was not kept for long.

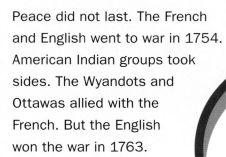

THINK ABOUT IT

Why did the Wendats and Tiontontati form a new nation? What would be the benefits of joining an existing nation such as the Ottawas instead?

Slaves and Servants Find Hard Lives

Work was hard to find in England in the early 1600s. People wanted to go to the colonies. But many could not afford the trip. So they became indentured servants. Criminals could be forced to become indentured servants.

Indentured servants served a master for four to seven years. They could be traded or sold to a different master. After their time was done, they were free. They might be given land. Lots of servants died before gaining their freedom.

In Virginia and Maryland, servants found hard work as tobacco hands. The crop required heavy labor. Fields needed tending. Leaves had to be harvested and processed. Farmers needed new fields cleared. Servants were overworked. They faced diseases and a harsh climate. When masters acted cruelly, the courts sided with them.

A servant (right) waits on a wealthy Dutch family.

100,000

Approximate number of English, Scottish, and Irish people who moved to tobacco areas in the 1600s.

- People became indentured servants to come to the New World.
- Both servants and slaves lived hard lives in Virginia.
- Over time, more colonists used slavery.
- The lives of slaves worsened.

While servants were treated badly, people who were enslaved were legally the property of their master. The first slaves in Virginia were American Indians. Later, colonists brought black people who were first enslaved in the Caribbean. Unlike servants, slaves did not choose to come to Virginia. Enslaved people lived hard lives in poor conditions. Early on, some were freed after serving a number of years. Others managed to buy their own freedom, but most could not.

By the late 1600s, fewer people in England were willing to be servants. Colonists began to rely heavily on slavery. But they feared the enslaved people might revolt. New laws limited the freedom of all black people. The lives of enslaved people got even harder. Their workdays became longer. They were given less food and medicine.

CAPTIVES

For some American Indian tribes, taking captives from other nations or colonies was important. Most often, these captives served one of two purposes. Sometimes the captives were used as revenge. Tribe members who had lost family members during conflicts could take out their anger on the captives. Some were tortured to death. Other times, the captives were adopted into the tribe. They took the place of tribe members who had died and were expected to act and dress like them.

21

Puritans Value Independence

The Puritans were a religious group started in England. They wanted to reform the Church of England. But many Puritans were unhappy with life in England. They thought the Church of England had not changed enough. In the 1630s, they saw a chance to create a new society in New England. They called the town they founded Boston.

In Europe, there was not a lot of free land. There was much competition among Europeans. Puritans saw New England as full of opportunities. But farming the land was not easy. The climate was colder than Virginia. Rocks

Puritans also tried to convert American Indians to their religion.

14,000

Approximate number of English Puritans who moved to New England in the 1630s.

- English Puritans saw the chance to be independent in New England.
- Puritans made laws and struggled over religion.
- England reduced the political power of the Puritans in New England.

Near Salem, Massachusetts, a group of Puritan girls accused more than 20 people of being witches.

dotted the soil. The Puritans did not mind. They thought hard work made them better people.

The Puritans formed their own government in New England. They passed laws based on the Bible. They formed their own churches. But not all Puritans agreed on how to create a kingdom of God.

The arguments over religious practices and beliefs grew messy. Some fled the colony. Others were banned. The Puritans also feared the devil and witches. Accused witches who did not confess could be hanged. After 1660, the English king began to take political control of New England away from the Puritans.

Wampanoags and Narragansetts Fight for Their Land

Native communities throughout New England formed connections with one another through rituals and marriage. Some clusters of villages were led by powerful men or women. The Wampanoags and Narragansetts were two such groups.

The arrival of Europeans in New England brought smallpox and other diseases. So many people died that some tribal communities were abandoned. English Puritans took over an old Wampanoag village to found Plymouth.

The Wampanoags allied with Plymouth. In return, they expected help keeping their land. Instead, they lost land to English settlers. In 1675, settlers in Plymouth killed three Wampanoags. Wampanoags began attacking farms. Colonists organized to defend their settlements. The two sides clashed, and the conflict spread. It became known as King Philip's War, after the Wampanoags' leader.

Other nations were affected. Some colonists saw all American Indians as their enemies. They attacked the powerful Narragansetts. Angry, the Narragansetts entered the war.

Colonists attack the Narragansetts' fort during King Philip's War.

3,000

Approximate number of American Indians killed in King Philip's War.

- The settlers of Plymouth took Wampanoag land and killed some tribe members.
- The Wampanoags, under King Philip, wanted revenge.
- Other nations took sides in the conflict.
- The groups fighting the colonists lost the war.

They fought against the colonists. At first, King Philip's men found it easy to get around the English. They attacked and destroyed many settlements.

Some tribes, such as the Pequots and the Haudenosaunee Confederacy, allied with the colonists. The war lasted more than a year. The Narragansetts, Wampanoags, and their allies lost. Many American Indians on both sides had died. The losers became enslaved or were scattered. The English took over more land.

THINK ABOUT IT

Why did some tribes help the colonists? What did they stand to gain?

European painting of King Philip

25

Pueblo People Find Common Ground

In the dry Southwest, some tribes of American Indians lived in pueblos. These were villages of stone and brick. The Pueblo people, such as the Zunis and Hopis, shared similar customs. They practiced the same style of farming. They danced in similar ceremonies. They worshiped in underground rooms.

But the Pueblo people were not united. They spoke several different languages. Each community ruled itself. When Spanish soldiers invaded in the late 1500s, several Zuni pueblos joined together to resist. A different town called Pecos wanted to ally with the Spanish. The town asked for help fighting a rival.

Spain established colonies among the pueblos. They forced the Pueblo people to give up their own culture and religion. They demanded food and goods from the Pueblo people and made them work in mines. These demands continued despite famine, disease, and war.

The Pueblo people saw the Spanish as a common enemy. The tribes united in 1680. They pushed out

A Zuni pueblo, photographed in the early 1900s

the colonists. They restored their own places of worship. But they also began fighting among themselves. Famine and attacks from outside tribes increased.

The Spanish won back many of the pueblos. This time, the Pueblo people were not forced to work or provide goods. They could also practice some of their own religion. The Pueblo people and the Spanish colonists fought together against outside enemies, such as the Utes and Apaches.

Today, many Zuni people live near Gallup, New Mexico.

7
Number of known languages spoken by the Pueblo people.

- Pueblo groups ruled themselves, despite sharing similar cultures.
- Spanish colonists forced the Pueblo people to give them food and work in mines.
- The Pueblo people revolted against the Spanish.
- The Pueblo people eventually fought alongside Spanish colonists against other enemies.

IMPOSING ALLIES

When the Spanish first invaded, they brought American Indian allies from Mexico with them. The Pueblo people had likely never come into contact with these people before. Along with Spanish soldiers, hundreds of Aztecs and other Mexican warriors marched into the pueblos. They used wooden swords. The swords had stone edges. The Aztecs wore feathered capes and held feathered shields.

27

Missions Spread Spanish Empire to California

In the 1500s, Spain held a large empire from South America to Mexico. Spanish explorers had grown rich by taking away gold and other valuables from local tribes. Unsatisfied with their wealth, the explorers traveled north from Mexico. They looked for new riches in the southern United States.

At first, the Spanish left California mostly alone. The American Indians they encountered were poor in the eyes of the Spanish. They had few precious metals or valuable trade goods. The tribes there did not grow corn, which the Spanish would have taken for food.

In the 1700s, Spain began to fear attacks from other countries. The Russians might invade California from the north. The English could come from the east. The Spanish wanted colonies to protect what they saw as their possession.

Not many Spanish colonists wanted to settle in these areas. So Spain encouraged missions. Missions are settlements focused on spreading a religion. The Spanish missions were funded by the Catholic Church. They did not cost the government of Spain

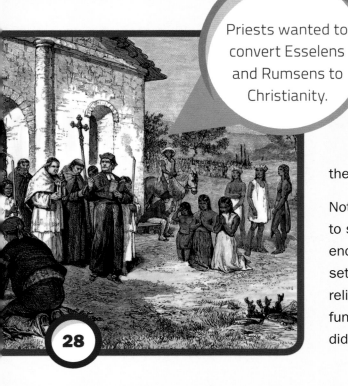

Priests wanted to convert Esselens and Rumsens to Christianity.

Mission Carmel was founded in California in 1770.

much. The missions spread Spanish culture as well as religion.

In California, priests tempted tribes to join their missions. They displayed religious art to convince local tribes of the power of Christianity. They offered trade goods, livestock, and crops.

But once American Indians joined missions, priests demanded they grow food for the church. Some were forced to build more missions. American Indians sometimes ran away from the missions. They were punished severely if caught.

1
Average number of days it took to travel between Spanish missions in California.

- Spanish explorers marched north from Central America and Mexico, looking for precious metals.
- Spain wanted to secure California from claims by Russia or England.
- Spain used missions instead of colonists to spread Spanish control to California.

THINK ABOUT IT

What makes something valuable? Do you think gold and silver will always be considered valuable?

Glossary

ally
A person or group on the same side of a conflict.

captive
A person who is taken and held prisoner.

confederacy
A union or group of people under the same leadership.

execution
The planned killing of a person, usually for a crime.

profit
Money that is gained by a person or business after all costs and expenses are paid.

pueblos
American Indian villages in the Southwest made of stone and clay.

ritual
A formal or religious event with actions performed in a specific manner.

smallpox
A disease from Europe that spread easily and caused rashes, fevers, and often death.

torture
To cause great pain or suffering.

unite
To join or work together.

For More Information

Books

Miller, Brandon Marie. *Women of Colonial America: 13 Stories of Courage and Survival in the New World*. Chicago: Chicago Review Press, 2016.

Raum, Elizabeth. *The Dreadful, Smelly Colonies: The Disgusting Details about Life during Colonial America*. Mankato, MN: Capstone Press, 2010.

Yasuda, Anita. *Traditional Stories of the Northeast Nations*. Minneapolis, MN: Abdo, 2017.

Visit 12StoryLibrary.com

Scan the code or use your school's login at **12StoryLibrary.com** for recent updates about this topic and a full digital version of this book. Enjoy free access to:

- Digital ebook
- Breaking news updates
- Live content feeds
- Videos, interactive maps, and graphics
- Additional web resources

Note to educators: Visit 12StoryLibrary.com/register to sign up for free premium website access. Enjoy live content plus a full digital version of every 12-Story Library book you own for every student at your school.

Index

About the Author

Clara MacCarald is a freelance writer with a master's degree in biology. She writes educational books for children. She has also written about news and science for local publications in central New York.